TO LOOK UPON EURYDICE

Kenneth Daniel Wisseman.

Copyright © 2024 by Kenneth Daniel Wisseman

All rights reserved.

No part of this book may be reproduced in any form or by any electronic or mechanical means, including information storage and retrieval systems, without written permission from the author, except for the use of brief quotations in a book review.

Cover, illustrations, and interior design by Kenneth Daniel Wisseman

ISBN: 979-8-9896411-1-6

❦ Created with Vellum

In loving memory of thy friendship,

My only true love,
Thou gav'st me the best memories of beauty
In the hours of my youth:—
Thou wert the love of my life.

TO LOOK UPON EURYDICE

A Collection of POEMS

BY

KENNETH DANIEL WISSEMAN

FIRST EDITION

ILLUSTRATED BY
KENNETH DANIEL WISSEMAN

CONTENTS.

TO LOOK UPON EURYDICE

PAGE

Preface XIII

I.—IDYLS OF LOVE

In Unreality	3
Starless Whisper	4
A Deeper Mystery	9
Solitude	12
The Wind When it Howls	14
Snowflakes	15
Transparent Thoughts	16
The Handiwork of Light	19
Living Waters	20

Echoes in Space	21
The End of Days	22
'Neath Willows Sorrowed	23

II.—LAMENTS OF LOSS

Truly I Loved But Thee	31
The Missing	32
Dreams of You	35
Though Drowned	36
Our Last	37
My Hearts a Shell	38
Unfriended Hour	40
Amber Rays	41
In the Wailing Tempest	42
No Tears for Me	43
To See Again	45
My Sweet Delores	46
Bright One	47
Her Dark Reflection	48
Rejection	54
This Rustic Place	55
The Piper's Song	56
Greener Were the Thoughts	57
In Drear Ennui	58

III.—TALES OF LORE

Sonnet to Thea 63
Helen 64
The Sound of Autumn 67
His Paradise 73
Isadora 74
Asphodel 79
Cleopatra and Her Antony 83

Epilogue 90

Acknowledgments 91

LIST OF ILLUSTRATIONS.

Self Portrait	II
Eurydice	8
Way of the Mono Trail	18
"The tender waters so softly caught her the heavens daughter"	25
"Only in dreams that hue of yestreen year"	34
"My broken heart's a shell and you my pearl"	39
"How shall these scribbled lines to yours compare in beauty"	44
"In a dream of an evening once 'neath cedar's emerald leaf"	53
"The popples pall where flowed our yestreen bond"	59
Helen of Troy	66
"In paradise his paradise was her"	72
Isadora	78
Cleopatra	89

Preface

Throughout my life, usually during times of great loss, or out of a feeling of great love, I would put a few lines of words down on paper, scribbles really. Those thoughts would be few and far between. And never did I write in structured verse, though I always had an admiration for this style of poetry. I remember as a young boy my mother gave me a small volume of English poetry. And it was in that book I came across the words of my favorite poet of all time, Lord Byron. His way of writing lyrical verses of love seemed, to me, to flow off the tongue better and be more memorable than the countless other poets, whom only later in my life would come to admire as well. Poets like Shelley and Keats. And American poets too, especially Edgar Allan Poe and Henry Wadsworth Longfellow. Such poets have been a great influence on my writing style.

 I am one to go against the advice never to use thee or thou or other archaic terms. But I seek beauty alone in my work, or at least what I find beautiful. I find that the use of older words tends to, on occasion, lend to better end-rhyming, and that reducing my vocabulary to only modern words limits me greatly as a wordsmith. However, I believe there has to be a delicate balance between the old and the new so that the reader can grasp the meaning of my poetry: too much of the arcane is something I try to avoid, especially in more lengthy poems. Although, other poets like Poe and Keats would make great use of an occasional archaic word, something I admire greatly about their work.

Meter was always my weakness as a poet, though rhyming, even as a child was something that felt quite natural to me. I cannot imagine writing a poem without at least internal rhymes, even if those rhymes are unintentional. When writing they can come to me at any time, even when I'm not sitting down with the intent to write a poem. And when they do I scribble down a few lines on scraps of paper and put them aside to be further developed, when I have time to sit down and contemplate, usually while listening to music. I have even had rare moments in dreams when the verses come to me, and have woken up to write down whatever I remember of those forgotten fragments.

Though all of these poems are written in classical forms, some are based on my early attempts at poetry, originally written in more modern vers libre: hence, a few modified versions of those thoughts, reflect my current style of writing. I find that just a few free verse lines give me more than enough inspiration to write many lines of structured verse and serve well as a rough outline: since, for me at least, end-rhyming lines tend to lead to more lines of thought in order to complete the rhyme scheme, directions of thought I otherwise would never have been led to without end-rhyme as a guideline. Thus, oddly enough, confinement to rules leads to more creativity. Such was the case with "Helen," a poem inspired by a fragment of free-verse I kept in my closet collecting dust, something I wrote going back who knows how long ago. Perhaps in that regard, it is my oldest poem, though my dedication and epilogue contain lines that may go back even further, and both have great meaning to me, hence serve as bookends to this, my first published work.

My lines went through many revisions: often I would go back to read some of my older poems and spot numerous flaws. This was particularly the case after having written so many lines of pentameter for a much larger work, which helped shape my poetic voice greatly. So, for now, I'm sending this smaller book of poems out into the world. It is my hope that these poems are enjoyed as an art form, one perhaps lost and forgotten about in the 20th century, save for a few poets like Robert Frost. For, I find the greatest beauty and enjoyment in writing such verse, and hope others enjoy reading the scribbled lines of this, my lesser works of poetry.

California, September, 2023

TO LOOK UPON EURYDICE

I
Idyls of Love

" Like leaves too soon to sear
That note upon the lyre"

— Kenneth

IN UNREALITY.

Prelude to 'Idyls of Love.'

DEEP in sleep, in a vision stark,
    When the world becomes so still and dark,
    Their amber flicker, beckoning sweet,
In half remember'd dreams we meet
Under Cynthia glowing above,
There, again in the eyes of love.
    In unreality's fleeting stare
As the owl resounds its mournful cries,
    Illumes her locks of golden hair,
'Tis here in her brown and balmy eyes,
In my dreams—my dream forever lies.

STARLESS WHISPER.

ENFOLD me love whilst parting,
    Pause time within thine arms,
The hour of dusk just starting,
    The stars within thy charms,
Their ling'ring glow I leer;
    My dream in twilight mire
Those eyes of amber mere,
    Which flow in liquid fire.

OF LOVE

Upon the witching ponder,
    Awake in dreams of thee,
Mine heart grows ever fonder
    Beneath that ever tree:
Where kithed our sacred air,
    The bliss of our embrace,
Plain o'er nigh willowed lair
    As last beheld thy face.

To quake thy lips with pleasure
    What Time has spilt with woe,
That drink of Love's sweet measure
    That I will never know:
Like leaves too soon to sear
    That note upon the lyre,
That oft decants a tear,
    The green to redden fire.

Below those leaves of sorrow
    Mine heart to thee I gave,
Though Love belies the morrow
    Betwixt the Muses stave;
Thy reverie I bear
    What ne'er these eyes will grace:
For in sweet lulls repair
    The Nine ensky thy face.

TO LOOK UPON EURYDICE

In this wood was pour'd that vase,
    We drank its sacred mixture,
In this glade our secret place
    Once filled with Love's elixir:
In this wine so otherwhere,
    Which press'd from lips suspire
What held from youthful prayer,
    Those whisper'd words of fire.

A loss yet lingers here
    When all of nature chills
And heard that starless whisper
    Upon the heart it stills:
Those words too soon lies bare
    Whose eyes too soon to trace,
Whose hair as Venus fair,
    Who stood before my face.

To touch that silvery dart
    Of Love too far to fain,
To hear another's heart,
    The sigh of lover's strain;
Whose wound unscathèd sears
    The leaves upon the pyre
As sheds the poet's tears:
    His letters lunt to fire.

OF LOVE

In the sound of Morpheus
    Where lover's song was stelled,
Lays the harp of Orpheus,
    Whom Sirens lulling stilled:
The Nightingale I hear
    As the stringèd lyre of Thrace,
That dulcet rime so dear,
    The beauty of your face.

The green of love's first vesper,
    Before the fragrant flower,
A still and starless whisper,
    Love's unrequited dour:
That fowl on boughs reveres
    That lonely note's desire,
Which wets the cheek with tears,
    Beneath selenic fire.

Below that twinkling sound,
    Upon a shooting star
With wishing whispers round,
    Lift loving eyes afar:
And hold me 'gain so near
    In this our trysting place;
And wipe away that tear:
    For Love has touch'd thy face.

January 27, 2019

TO LOOK UPON EURYDICE

Eurydice

OF LOVE

A DEEPER MYSTERY.

A Deeper mystery softly lics
In the color of her darkened eyes,
A tawny shade of autumn's glade,
The last sweet sate 'fore seasons fade;
'Twas here among the timbers fair,
The last I saw her timid stare;
Fore'er I love and ne'er forget
That girl! the day the last we met
'Twas though she knew ne'er fain again,
Mine eyes to sate—her eyes retain;
Yet here in dreams my love still lies
In sylvan shade and darkened eyes.

'Twas sweet suasion's still emote,
Which our wist—so softly wrote
Without a sigh nor single word,
The flatt'ring feign of love unheard;
That ling'ring lilt shall ne'er depart,
Fore'er sweet poesy on my heart:

TO LOOK UPON EURYDICE

For when the soul beholds the eyes,
A limn whose light sheds tears and cries,
That lilting glass, so lucent cast,
Reflects our bosom long at last;
O pond'rous heart of mine be still!
Thy mirror pores on like a rill,
Thy beam a sea of sounding deeps,
Where the arching willow weeps:
A pool where Echo soft replies,
Lost without her darkened eyes—

Yet what with words thou nigh conceived,
My soul surmised, nigh half perceived:
For like a brook which gently flows,
Meanders memories' sweeten'd throes;
As for my troth to thee I sing,
Thy face, thy form, a nocturnal spring:
A vision seen as Luna glows,
Thy shape a shade in sweet repose,
'Twined in mine arms so fairly brace;
O woe! the sight of parting face,
That here by brook would ne'er awake,
Fore'er to sate, thy sigh partake:
The kiss which lingers ends too soon,
Our fates unknown, be bane or boon;
Allured by love 'low starry skies,
'Low willows arch and darkened eyes.

OF LOVE

O deep that drink mine eyes imbibe
What lilt of lips can ne'er describe;
A look of Love the Fates forbade,
Thy cast a hint of seasons fade;
Though near to me, thy glance afar
As 'bove the sea, my guiding star;
" Alas! No more," the Stars entreat,
Their song 'twas stay'd where last we meet;
And on my bower afore I sleep,
I pray for thee with tears I weep;
Thy name the last of sighs—a kiss—
Upon the hush of heaven's abyss:
O may fain be her bosom fair,
Which beat for me 'neath cedarn air,
A place of dreams where love still lies
'Neath emerald leaf—and darkened eyes.

March 27, 2017

SOLITUDE.

There stills a silent roar amidst the wold,
    Where pours the alabaster waterfalls
    To stone a-hewn immortal, nature's hold,
    And strings her harp within its crystal walls:
    A world without the lying lyre, and all's
    Solitude—here that timid maiden hides—
    In torrent of mist, soft her echoed calls;
    She bathes within the brooklet's tender tides,
Her voice alone which balms the wound my heart confides.

The fragrant airs of incense cedar looms,
    A mem'ry dear, dearworth of yesteryear;
    Adrift on wintry wind those sweet perfumes
    To soothe vail'd boughs o'er pool of green veneer,
    Those sorrowful sand sallows drooped awry:
    For nature 'dures the curse of fallen man,
    In solitude, redemption is her cry;
    In reveries of when the Stars began
To sing, before foreshorten'd hour of mortals span.

OF LOVE

Below the high Sierra's cloudy lift
    There haunts the song of winter's iv'ry spell,
    A certain coldness—'tis her love adrift,
    A netherworld which stills the highland fell,
    Which fathoms fain the hill, the rill and dale;
    And eerie is the waters quietude
    On mornings tender glow, her whiten'd veil,
    Preludes of joy!—from bosom'd tears exude;—
In nature lone, alone not I—in Solitude.

                                        March 10, 2021

TO LOOK UPON EURYDICE

THE WIND WHEN IT HOWLS.

The howling wind wakes leaves of yellow,
   Sweetly moaning an Omen dinn'd,
Orison's intoned words rebellow
   The howling wind.

   Cold is her brace no charms within,
Turned the green to waning mellow,
   Seasons' thoughts of what could have been.

Love yet lingers, in her hands the arrow,
   Touches tenderly on the mind,
Playing sweetly her enchanting cello,
   The howling wind.

April 22, 2020

SONNET.

Snowflakes.

Like thoughts they linger on the chilly air,
Adrift on austral rays of slanted light,
Where all the world's a silent otherwhere,
An alabaster ever veil'd in white.
On wings descend to cedar, pine and oak;
And fall a shooting star o'er hill and plain,
Where's heard a whisper'd wish on lips invoke,
Whose sigh re-echoes yesteryear's refrain.
'Tis but the drop of heaven's icy tear!
Laments of Stars from skiey clime of clouds,
Which fall to earth on whiten'd winter's year;
A Sprite, whose spell the crystal dust enshrouds.
    His brightness falls on what was once so green:
    The leam of Love—on woods idyllic scene.

December 25, 2019

SONNET.

Transparent Thoughts.

The drifting dour of mist enveils the hill,
    Afloods the vale angelic rays alight,
    Where waters kiss the sky, a heavenly sight,
    This solitude of oak and crystal rill;
The sun retires below the mauvish frill
    Of clouds as the moon lifts to lofty height,
    The daystar quench'd, that torch of golden light,
    Yet on Diana's face it flickers still,
Whose beauty drew Endymion's soft sigh
    At night. For Love's a maid in white sateen,
    Transparent thoughts, which words will never 'tice,
A nectar'd air, which Nature fills the eye
    As 'twere a parchment's yellow'd could have been,
    Her lines in reverie of paradise.

April 22, 2020

Way of the Mono Trail

OF LOVE

THE HANDIWORK OF LIGHT.

Through meadow'd wood the sound so still
   Of streamlet starts to spell its rime,
   Where once I stood in yestertime,
The scent of pine, unquench'd its fill.

Love through the bowers bathes benight,
   Upon the winding trail its play,
   Alone am I, and yet this ray
Reveals the handiwork of Light.

And like a youthful dream I knew,
   This little wood which leads me on,
   A wistful song in Babylon,
The mountain lake commands my view.

August 21, **2022**

SONNET.

Living Waters.

Amongst the woodland hills and sounding shore
   Is heard the hush of restful interlude;
   And I repose in restful solitude,
   Where green of love is felt forevermore.
Beside the lily pond my ponder pore,
   'Way from the turbulence of Time's intrude,
   'Neath high Sierra skies the heart renewed,
   In wistful wonder by the brooklet's roar.
From out the woods the free and bonny hart,
   The forest fawn to silvery waters led,
   In sylvan shade she's safe from hunters dart;
O, blissful still by stilly fountainhead!
   My fragile heart is ever fonder here,
   A vessel cleansed by Living Waters clear.

December 6, 2019

SONNET.

Echoes in Space.

Aneath her blue-lit veil the gossamer moon,
Adrift above the clouds that wandering belle;
And in a pensive pause, with heart aswoon
See clear the touch of Love's supernal spell.
To feel the yellow sun upon my skin,
To see the dark a brighter ray assay,
To hear the sprite of Spring sibylline,
The haunting skylark's sounding roundelay.
O Earth! in black abyss, what hand has wrought
The daffodil, that flow'r thy children pluck?
And with a sigh give haste to wishful thought,
With eyes so innocent and eyes awestruck.
   Echoes in space, the dark dimm'd, bask'd so bright:—
   An azure jewèl formed by voice of Light.

November **16**, **2019**

SONNET.

The End of Days.

A LONELY cricket chirps a ballad brusque,
On hedge of field the gleaners go to sleep;
The sun goes down o'er western skies at dusk,
Above the seven sisters of the deep.
Return'd those little sprites upon the flower
To home of comb and lonesome creviced stone,
The bee and butterfly upon that hour
When Artemis reposes on her throne.
The twilight stood as 'twere a tearful maid
In samite robes upon the saffron field;
On me—her darkling eyes so plaintive laid,
The rays of day her raiment could not shield.
   The end of days unveils a mistress rare
   To rest my weary head on bosom fair.

November 10, **2019**

OF LOVE

'NEATH WILLOWS SORROWED TREE.

'NEATH willows sorrowed
   Love's dart was arrowed
   By beauty mellowed
      A sight unseen;
   Her head 'twas pillowed
   On flowers haloed
   In bower willowed
      My sweet undine!
   Yet lulled to sweven
   That vernal even
   Nigh springs artesian,
      From susurrate earth,
   'Low starry vailed
   Cascades reveled
In violet blooms, embosomed mirth.

   Her golden tresses
   Perfume yet blesses,
   Sweet evanescences
      In fragrant blush:
   A thousand presses
   Of soft caresses,
   In violet, dresses

TO LOOK UPON EURYDICE

  Her form—so lush;
 The leaves a-quaking
 For love awaking,
 Yet green with aching;
  Ah! sweet perfume,
 Those deep'ning fringes
 Above as tinges
Her cheeks as roses youthful bloom.

  And as she dozes
 Below reposes,
 In dreams of roses;
  Amidst her hair
 The air encloses
 And there composes,
 In soft transposes,
  A song so fair;
 O Zephyrus!
 Knows she's the fairest,
 A maiden rarest,
  So leesome shown,
 Her tresses golden
 As Venus olden,
From heights above, abandoned throne.

  The tender water
 So softly caught her
 The heavens daughter:

OF LOVE

Her image shone
As ever after,
Love's starry wander,

TO LOOK UPON EURYDICE

A mirrorèd wonder,
    The mere her throne;—
There'pon our parting,
The waves a-darting,
I'll still be doting
    Her foamèd wake:
With tears a-shaking,
My heart a-breaking,
I'll see her stilly on the lake.

The bosom swelling
So balmy telling
Her dreams a-dwelling
    In heaving breast;
So sweet their quelling,
No doomèd knelling,
No tears a-welling,
    A tranquil rest;
Whilst soothing sounding
Of rills abounding,
Their air a-rounding
    Her 'ticing charms;—
Upon her arousing
Will she be cowering?
This fey enchantress—in mine arms.

In dreams a-shivering
Of mirror shimmering
Her bosom clinging

OF LOVE

To Morpheus!
With eyes a-twinkling
Yet half awakening
'Neath Love a-wandering,
    Fair Vesperus;
To me she claspeth
As kohlèd lashes
Upon me flashes;
    Her eyes a-leam
Yet lingers raptured,
A vision captured,
" O sweetling—tell me of thy dream."

    Ah! blushet, blushing
With looks so loving,
The heart a-rushing;
    An ivory neck
And cheek a-flushing,
The smile a-gushing
The wilds a-hushing.—
    With looks that beck
So fain a beam soft,
Which drawls a sweet soft
Her sighs enthrall soft,
    " My dream was thee,
By water aflow,
The clouds a pillow,
Reposed 'neath willows sorrow'd tree."

July 26, 2018

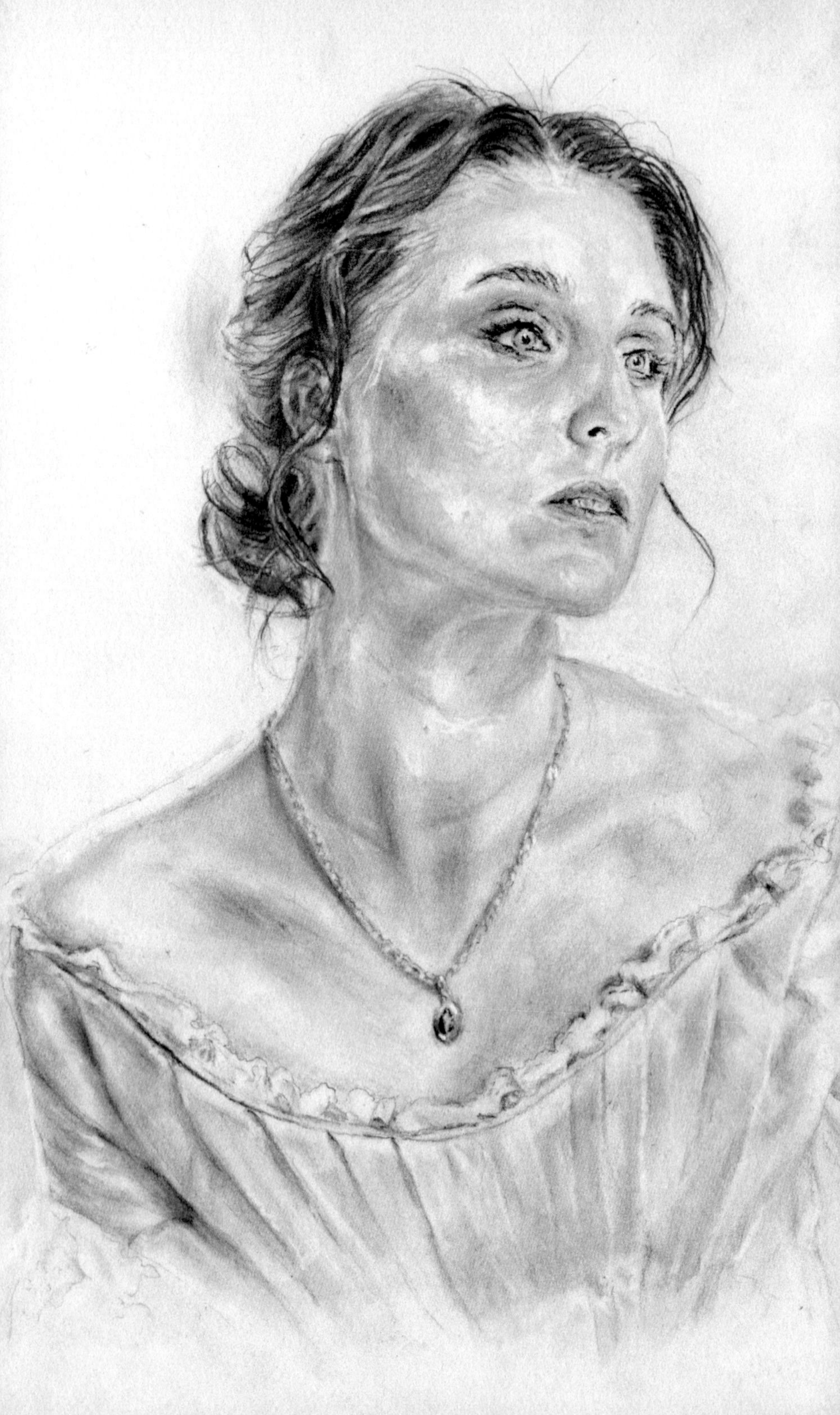

II

Laments of Loss

" Only in dreams that hue of yestreen year,
    That season poured with poems true my vow"

— Kenneth

TRULY I LOVED BUT THEE.

Prelude to 'Laments of Loss.'

TRULY I loved but thee, my princess fair
   And, in the twilight hour, when rests the jay
   Under the eaves, and crickets strum the air,
'Tis thee that Morpheus shows me clear as day.
And, in that little spell of sleep thy crown
Of hair still golden with no streaks of gray,
Untied, a flowing rivulet falls to ground;
To wipe away the tear that trickles down
Thine aspect smiling gay, my love with eyes of brown.

THE MISSING.

THE clock is ticking on the sanguine wall,
   So weirdly was our sylvan meeting then,
   That pathway golden led to cedar tall;
Oh! 'twas our everlasting rest, that glen,
Though dappled where those skies above the fen,
The ray arrayed within your eyes–amour;
Why, why I love you girl as I did then?
In winter's cold embrace I found a more—
Tender enchantment—eyes of brown—forevermore.

OF LOSS

Your liquid fire of amber stirr'd my heart,
    And youthful reveries came back to me
    As lost forgotten dreams—your stolen dart;
    Yet there reposed beneath that ever tree
    I saw what now wish fain these eyes could see,
    And felt at peace within your bosom pale;
    Above that red-tail'd hawk—he glided free—
    As 'twere the very pinion of Love's sail;—
But now, at night am left with wrack—and song to wail.

Those golden tresses, treasured by me now,
    Only in dreams that hue of yestreen year,
    That season poured with poems true my vow;
    And 'low the murky midnight moon, that sphere
    Which fills the lover's ling'ring wounds, a prayer
    For you I whisper each and every night,
    And wipe my emerald eyes, their wet repair.—
    Those locks now grey, my Eve in evening light;
My Muse, the one with ebony ink stains—I write.

The missing of you, two hearts beat as one:—
    Take me within your arms—pause Time—awhile
    Before we part and never see the sun
    Shine bright as it once did—your gentle smile;—
    Go t'ward your dreams, your eastern wone, and I'll
    Stay here upon these shores, this brooklet wild
    And bathe within its chill—your love's denial,
    Remembering thoughts fain of eyes so mild—
With laughter's gaiety, my sweetling—forest child.

February 9, 2021

OF LOSS

" Only in dreams that hue of yestreen year"

DREAMS OF YOU.

I'm lost in tender dreams of you,
   In reveries mine heart doth ache;
   And though the light of morrow break,
Shines bright upon idyllic view,

Mine heart still pierced by dart you drew;
   Mine eyes grow wet with tearful wake,
I'm lost in tender dreams of you,
   In reveries mine heart doth ache.

O faery girl with eyes of blue,
   The wound is deep of your forsake!
   Go pour a potion to unmake
My love, with root of mandrake brew—
I'm lost in tender dreams of you.

January 17, 2021

TO LOOK UPON EURYDICE

THOUGH DROWNED.

Knowing a once and perfect form of love
    That shone beneath these lattice leaves of green,
    Whose shadows shaded us, the memory of
    The little lapping pool, its sapphire sheen;
    And you my first true love, my woodland queen,
    That day, or dream, or something else I think,
    A breath of life within idyllic scene,
    Where once by beauty stole its amber drink,
Though drown'd within your eyes, would sail again its brink.

May **21, 2022**

OUR LAST.

WHY was the day so short yet somehow long
As 'twere the ceaseless ever of a song
Unheard until our parting woke its rhyme?
The chorus out of dreams, our little time
Together—when for just a space—to walk—
Beneath the dark arcade, and had our talk,
Our peace—our broken glass of youthful past:
Our sweet repast of memories sweet—our last.

February **15, 2023**

TO LOOK UPON EURYDICE

SONNET.

My Heart's a Shell.

O how Dyane sings soft soliloquy,
A sweet lament to lull the troubled soul;
And glides upon the sea a symphony,
Where'pon the Stars of Heaven walk the shoal.
Eternal prints along the secret cove,
Where once we two had walked as lovers new,
And the night-winds embraced our form and wove
Her tapestry with blue heartstrings of woo.
O what's this thing called love, what waxèd make?
That draws the Muse upon the lips of breath,
And churns the waters deep abyss to break
The heart, whose waning tide's the kiss of death?
   O moonlit treasure wing'd to sandy whirl,
   My broken heart's a shell—and you my pearl.

September 27, 2020

OF LOSS

"My broken heart's a shell and you my pearl"

SONNET.

Unfriended Hour.

DELIGHTED I within the sounding soft
That was your lilt, which held me closely then;
With each slight pause I saw that star so oft,
That twinkled thought of shooting stars again.
And in your eyes beside the babbling brook
A deeper meaning lied within your note;
The ebb of Time belied your distant look,
Those dulcet deeps of haunting heart's emote.
Two friends yet now unfriended hour of pain;
O tell me why delighted we so brief?
The reveries of greener days remain,
A candle lit beside this yellow'd leaf.
   So short is life, with her I'd rather stay,
   A friendship lost, my Muse forsook away.

November 13, **2019**

SONNET.

Amber Rays.

THINE eyes of amber rays ashine anew
On this my bosom true—and, always fond
   Of thee, the way doth sweet my love abscond,
   As gold more precious held than sapphires blue.
One sun yet fills my days and dries the dew—
   Of sorrows pain, and draws my strings respond
   With sweet mellifluous daydreams beyond;
   One moon yet fills my nights—thy timid view.—
Bound to that one whom fills the nights within
   Thy breast, whilst I alone can only dream
   Of what sweet midnight songs are harbor'd in
Thy fathoms ebb, heart's dark and deep'ning stream
   Of love, the tender touch of lips to skin;
   Yet in thine eyes I see—what could have been.

                                      February 4, 2021

SONNET.

In the Wailing Tempest.

In starry twilight dreams again we meet,
The murky moonlight lit and fairily
    Touched soft thy face and form in ebbing sweet
    In pearly dress, aflow so airily;
Yet placid stood apart, where once the beat
    Of twain our aching hearts as one serene,
    Thine eyes so softly glowed an azure pool
    When last they filled my deeps of emerald green;
And in the wailing tempest, thoughts I'd often
    Ponder—and pine for thee, my lostling jewel!
    And die without those sapphire eyes to soften
My nights, and crestfallen the ocean's song:
    The heart persists when all's forgotten,
    Tenderness of love remains, when all is gone.

May **2, 2017**

OF LOSS

SONNET.

No Tears For Me.

Though try I might to write these verses fair,
In idle time, with reason'd thoughts alight,
How shall these scribbled lines to yours compare
In beauty? nay of lustre looming bright
Beyond the azure vault of heaven's reach;
Your light ever shining while I dream,
Outrays with every drop of lover's speech:
For, hers outpour on page, a crystal stream.
I, I am just—but dust, to dust shall go,
No flower'd laurel on my tomb to lay,
No tome inscribed to eyes of indigo,
Nor statue of my form, of great display,
    My words shall burn upon the highland lea,
    And drift unto the clouds—no tears for me.

February 28, **2023**

TO LOOK UPON EURYDICE

"How shall these scribbled lines to yours compare in beauty?"

TO SEE AGAIN.

To see again your eyes, so warm
Their mist of musing of a storm
   In Nature's bosom, where we dwelt
And drank of beauty's watery view,
The languid lake of crystal dew;
   Our love was one both seen and felt
   Within the spell
Of your gaze,
That cold and solitary day.
   See again your quivered lip,
Lay bare my breast upon a whim,
   My heart—for your companionship!
And, as your words reflect on him,
Will ever steal—with dark betray.

To see again your eyes so warm,
Before our parting sorrow'd storm.

February **26, 2023**

TO LOOK UPON EURYDICE

MY SWEET DELORES.

The rustle of the rubric leafs
   Leaves me with reverie
Of you upon the paths we walked
   'Neath sullen ivory.

The tra-la trilling of the sparrow
   Spares me the mournful threne
Of wellaway within your arms;
   And I remember when

Your sigh—the wind upon my face,
   Facing your questions rue,
And I so innocent of love,
   What I once held so true.

The white sun's warmth upon my brow,
   Brown eyes within this dream
As we a-rove the wintry path
   Along the silvern stream.

On spring day's bloom I feel the chill,
   Children of the forest
We were, and you my faery sprite,
   My light—my sweet Delores.

May 6, 2020

BRIGHT ONE.

O, GAZE bright one, your ray I see
Before my face, my dearworth flower,
And hidden 'tis, that treasure we
      Dreamt on bower.

My sweetling, distant star—shine bright—
With loving looks of skiey hue,
On evensong, before the night,
      I sing of you.

With locks of ringlets flowing o'er
Your lucent bosom down to ground,
My thoughts, my tears to you outpour
      Long deep's profound.

'Tis on these Orient shores was torn
This string, its fickle band of blood,
This soft heartstring which now doth morn—
      The eye—aflood.

February **6, 2021**

TO LOOK UPON EURYDICE

HER DARK REFLECTION.

In dreams in still of the evening light
   Of the dusk that is your deep,
In dreams I long for you at night,
And write with ink of your beauty's light
   From my heart with tears I weep!
      For our love of what was that once
      In memory's haunts, it seems,
      All that gleams in idyllic dreams:
My heart was stolen by her dark reflection.

I wander beneath the cool arcades
   Through places we once roved,
Aromas of verdant cedar shades
Yet fills my senses, Eden pervades;
   'Twas here I fell—and loved.—
      Inly sadness to glee at once;
      Forbidden your garden seems,
      All that gleams in idyllic dreams:
My heart was stolen by her dark reflection.

OF LOSS

That morning, as old friends we meet at last!
   By the streamlet saw the boon
Of your countenance fair! which cast
A spell, as we twain held fast
   In bosom basked in swoon.—
     'Twas there Time was stilled that once,
     In fathomed thought it seems,
     All that gleams in idyllic dreams:
My heart was stolen by her dark reflection.

That morning was shadowed by faery drear
   On our tryst along the bourn
'Neath pines perfumed austere;
We meandered 'round that mirrored mere
   We reposed 'neath willows lorn,
     My curtsied queen that once—
     Tears unforeseen it seems,
     All that gleams in idyllic dreams:
My heart was stolen by her dark reflection.

TO LOOK UPON EURYDICE

That morning we espied above the tree:—
   In veiled and vapoured blue
Soared a red-tailed hawk, so free;
Ah! 'twas Love's swift wings upon her and me,
   Those wistful beams which drew
     Then upon my heartstrings that once,
     Words wished—unsaid it seems,
     All that gleams in idyllic dreams:
My heart was stolen by her dark reflection.

To wander beneath a nebulous mist!
   Refrains yet that dulcet dart,
On the shore, where reposed your form on our tryst
'Neath lonesome lour, so far from your midst.
   Ah! why did you depart?
     O, sweet nymph to requite just once!
     My love—though you leave it seems,
     All that gleams in idyllic dreams:
My heart was stolen by her dark reflection.

OF LOSS

That eve on our walk's abandonment
   I sated long—your look;—
Our stars were fated 'bove the Orient
As we stood 'neath cedars viridescent.
   Above the willowed brook,
      Love's sweet susurrus sprang at once!
      A stream never stilled—it seems,
      All that gleams in idyllic dreams:
My heart was stolen by her dark reflection.

And your words, they haunt along this creek;
   And I weep for dreamèd things,
And in this vale 'tween two worlds bespeak
Where sorrow stilled on lilt's mystique;
   Where Love's arrow flew from wings!
      Where your stare was teared that once
      Last seeing mine eyes of green—
      All that glisters of gold serene!
My heart was stolen by her dark reflection.

TO LOOK UPON EURYDICE

Lost without you here amongst trees fair;
   Oft I go to those places deep
In our secret vale, where perfumed air
Of sweet cedars yet lingers dulcet there;
   And sometimes I smile and weep
      For you, an avision that once
      In reveries sleep—it all seems,
   All that gleams in idyllic dreams:
My heart was stolen by her dark reflection.

The willowed creek yet greets me meek
   I'm now changed from this—tender ache;
And walk alone bewet my cheek,
Another's gleam I shall not seek.
   To contemplate—awake!
      In a dream of an evening once
      'Neath cedar's emerald leaf—
   All that gleams!—is a tear of grief:——
My heart was stolen by her dark reflection.

April 21, **2018**

OF LOSS

" In a dream of an evening once 'neath cedar's emerald leaf "

TO LOOK UPON EURYDICE

REJECTION.

To sever friendship with a loomer's weave
    As like a tempest raging, Fate so cruel!
    Yet, so is life, the Earth before we leave,
    And we in ocean's deeps the meandering school
    Yet look upon this poppling silent pool:
    For, in its light the luminous fair face
    Of Love, whose beauty made a musing fool
    Of her, whose melodies surround this place,
Rejection's susurrus sweet, 'tis Echo's soft replies retrace.

May 30, **2022**

THIS RUSTIC PLACE.

A DAFFODIL within the wall,
A gust of wind above,
A tawa tree which gently sways,
    She plucks the flow'r with love;
        The rain
    Autumnal once again
        Allays
    Her 'panion there in pain,
Her soldier, one and all;
    She sings to him sweet lays.

Her eyes of gray recall
    A tale of forgotten love,
A smile yet grows upon the sight
    Of eyes, which gently rove
        The vase,
    Her touch in fond retrace;
        His sprite
    Within this rustic place,
Midst yellow blooms of evenfall,
    Recall'd her distant light.

January 12, **2020**

TO LOOK UPON EURYDICE

THE PIPER'S SONG.

I.

When thoughts of you are what remain,
   By faint, the patter of the rain,
I ponder on the love we had,
What Fate with silent words forbade
As Nature plays her music sad.

II.

To die within, without your touch
   Or semblance sweet, an ache too much!
The piper's song returns to me,
" Defy the Fates! their keen decree—
I wait for you—eternally."

III.

The dragonflies aflutter 'bout
   The fleeting shadow of a trout;
Does Nature know this loss I feel?
Endeavors ever like a wheel,
She blooms for love—what once was real.

February 26, 2023

GREENER WERE THE THOUGHTS.

Greener were the thoughts of you, that day
   The winds embraced the yellow willow bower,
   Whose tearful song entreated us to stay
   Reposed beside the lake, bespell'd that hour.
   Though Nature slept, no bloom of fullest flower,
   And cold the zephyr's breath and Time his touch,
   I'll ne'er forget what brighten'd all the dour!
   Beneath the cloudy sky, your eyes had such
A warm and tender light, no girl I'll love—as much.

May 22, 2022

SONNET.

In Drear Ennui.

ALONE in tears I sit in drear ennui,
    I loved her loneness and her azure eyes;
    I kneel and reverie those days when we
Took arms as lovers 'neath those smokey skies.
Without her bright amour and silvern dart,
I ride alone without my princess white,
The chantress of the quill and of my heart;
Her flame of fiery passion—quench'd that night.
My heroine now eyes another's worth,
Yet lives within my bosom, still her words,
Whilst looking fixed yon Luna's fiery hearth,
My Muse's echoed song of sylvan birds,
    " The popples pall where flowed our yestreen bond."
    And then she disappear'd with inky wand.

April 13, 2020

OF LOSS

" The popples pall where flowed our yestreen bond. "

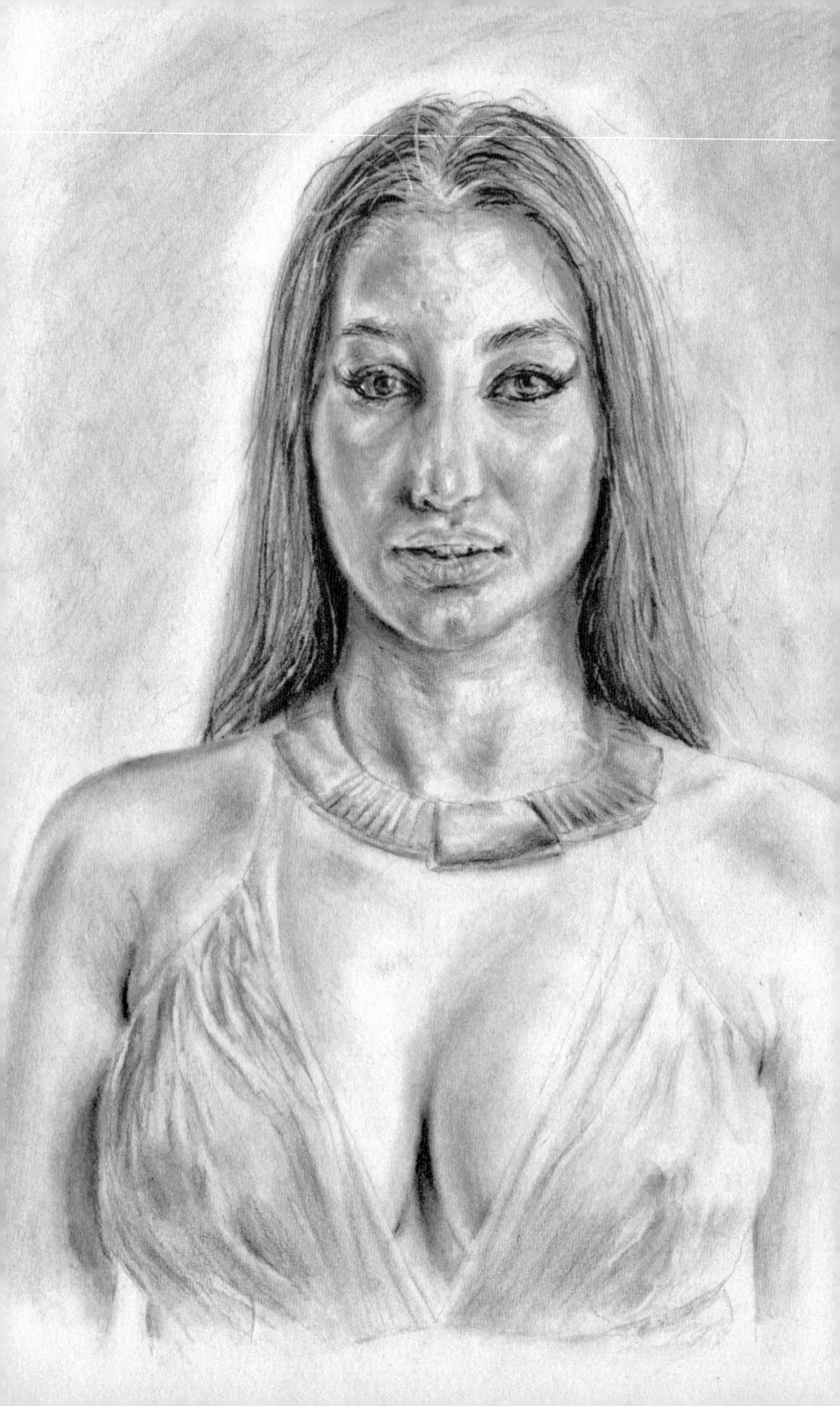

III
Tales of Lore

" Thou hast awaken the eyes of Greece,
   Thy face a thousand ships!"

— Kenneth

SONNET TO THEA.

Prelude to 'Tales of Lore.'

UPON a plinth there stood a statue proud
    Festoon'd with ivy twining there around
    Her lithy limbs and chained, her bosom bound—
Where once succor'd songs the vines enshroud
The air which sorrow sweet she did uncloud
With tenderness, that waning ray of smile,
Those sanguine lips a draught of warm beguile
To sate beneath the desert's dappled cloud.
The sages speak of thee upon thy tomb,
Unearthly is thy blacken marble hewn
As 'twere the shadow of thy light's relume,
Adrift the Nile beneath the Huntress Moon;
Her beauty roved these shores perfumed, one whom
The Roman viper vanquish'd far too soon.

HELEN.

O, saw ye not fair Helen?
    She's gone out from the west
   To dazzle in Love's rebellion,
    And rob the world of rest.

OF LORE

She sat upon an ivory throne,
    With her crown, not gild of gold
But shone as the dawning sea's enthrone
    Stolen rays of Love foretold.

Her eyes of emerald stole my heart,
    Emerald pools of an Orient shore;
Hair none of sable as Venus in art;—
    Our love of legend and lore.

Kissing Propontis pearls from the sea,
    And placing their string on her body
Whisper'd, " O my belovèd come with me
    For the night is full, the day not gaudy.

" O sable night full of dreams
    Like thousands seen afore!
Selene o'er salty sea agleams,
    Ferry us across that western shore."

O Spartan daughter!—a masterpiece
    Overlooking with trembling lips
Thou hast awaken the eyes of Greece,
    Thy face a thousand ships!

July 12, **2015**

TO LOOK UPON EURYDICE

Helen of Troy

OF LORE

THE SOUNDS OF AUTUMN.

I.

O SILENT season sate with colors cast
As flames, in wildwoods, last of summer's kiss
On leaves, a remembrance of all things past;

'Tween wintry winds, in stygian nights abyss,
And summer's light to Autumn's shadows turn
A deeper hue, 'tis then—it's you I miss;—

Memories of love like these leaves which burn
Aflame so red, a flame so brightly hued,
For you, in my twilight's sojourn, I yearn;

'Tis when I sit by waters quietude,
I hear your voice and see you dimly standin'
This time of year, in Nature's solitude:

O, how in nature miss you sweet companion,
When love awakes the leaves with sweet abandon!

TO LOOK UPON EURYDICE

II.

Amidst the still rivulet's rush, the sky,
Like softly-hued eyes staring down on me
A fairer shade of blue, her gaze so shy,

As on that day, that spring, we danced in glee
That Carolina e'en 'neath lightning's glance;
Aglisten'd her rain-drench'd skin so ivory,

A naiad of the woods, in wet entrance,
Bespell'd by all her charms, in arms adorn
Her countenance aglow in radiance

'Neath darken southern skies, like tears forlorn,
Dew on her fairy face aglow in love
That day, as when by Fates our love was born;

Now Autumn's wingèd winds from heav'n above
Send haunting howls of change, where once we rove.

OF LORE

III.

Remember that summer I spent with her,
'Twas here by brooklet fair for days, day long,
Long summer's glee, when time became a blur;

'Twas here we swam the pools till evensong
When we were young and sylvan woods our bower,
And you my tryst, my summer's dream, nightlong;

O, but our fate was torn that midnight hour!
I lowly born was deemed not mete by fate
Dark whispers, a death knell to friendship's flower:

O words, those words did pierce and devastate!
So soon she left, leaving me here in tears—
And sought with tears to reconciliate

With heartfelt letters sent that wintry year,
That year of sorrow and of sadness drear.

TO LOOK UPON EURYDICE

IV.

For many a moon, wander'd here alone,
As leaves which turn a deeper shade of red,
Love's yestereve, now lost in Time's unknown;

The seasons changed, yet I remained as dead,
Forlorn, without her seasons had no meaning,
Leaves changed her heart for nought, my words unread;—

All was an autumnal tone that evening,
The leaves aflame so brightly hued, a dream
I'll ne'er forget, she stood there breathless, leaning

'Neath naked oak as all the world agleam
Became anew aneath a golden shower
Of leaves, and bonny was her sunny beam;

As we embraced that sweet reunion hour,
Beneath that tree first kiss'd my dearworth flower.

OF LORE

V.

Aswoon'd at the sight of my bonny boon!
Again we fell in love, for e'er to cleave
With plight of trothed lips;—for many a moon

The seasons had meaning—again to me—
On certain autumnal dawns before the eve
Of winter's sleep, I'd lean 'neath that oak tree

With sated colors cast and gather its leaf;
Spring was her season, mine was always fall,
And as the tears fell down, 'twas there—I'd grieve;—

The early pink of spring, loved most of all,
Only one blossom lingers now abloom,
Like she adorn'd to the autumnal ball,

Leaves change, yet love, it alters not its tune—
A rose with golden leaves—lay on her tomb.

July 29, 2016.

TO LOOK UPON EURYDICE

" In paradise his paradise was her "

SONNET.

His Paradise.

When Eden bloom'd with flower'd air divine,
And evening drew the song of sweet opine,
The warbler note amidst the fruitful bower,
No sound of sorrow—in that golden hour.
Beside the stilly pool, a meadow'd place,
The breeze would blow upon his chisel'd face;
Upon its mirror'd waters he would stare
And dream of her, would see her pearly glare.
When he awoke that morning, all was bright:
For, in the mist arose in mellow light
The dream he dreamt, his treasure shaped so fair,
The woman lustred in the dewy air—
In Paradise—his—paradise was her,
The matchless beauty—bath'd in drifting myrrh.

February 24, 2023

TO LOOK UPON EURYDICE

ISADORA.

Nigh a lonely cypress which stood upon the height
    Of the ocean far above the tiding shore,
Wind-blown remains of a seaward wight,
    White-stones now fallen, yet o'er the roar;
They sing of an Eden within that hem
    Now bound by baneful briars and dwale
There'pon the salty air drifts that dulcet hymn
        O'er the gale.

Waves swash below the wuthering tor
    And lave the shores of that lonely island,
Where was prest the prints which bore
    The mark of lovers in saraband;
Whose feet once drew upon this steep,
    Whose gaze once grew towards the east,
Whose cheek once dew'd with tears to weep,
        When love ceased.

OF LORE

The ruined way winds 'bove the spray
    Towards that once eternal tree,
To shade the glade once filled with the lay
    Of a far and distant sea;
'Twas here he planted the rose adorn'd,
    Surround he raised a wall of stone;—
Yet Time's interment arose the thorned
        Weeds alone.

O, nary an airstone wish from a petal to pluck:
    For laughter and flower the air no more to fill
With sweet strains—from the brambly vine falls not the laverock
    In idyll, nor the nocturnal chant of the whippoorwill:
For what's idyll without a rose
    Pressed on the songbird's breast to lull
In sonnet?—O'er sandy leas echoes
        A seagull.

The Orient orb and skiey tears
    Withers dead a lonely lingering blush,
Her faint perfume soon disappears—
    Seaward rue brings Zephyrus to hush:
Reveries when gaiety bloom'd in round,
    Almaining hither 'neath skies that redden,
Drawing lovers eyes yon illumed profound
        East of Eden.

TO LOOK UPON EURYDICE

Hand in hand twain souls overlooking the deep;
    Was her heart full of muse to her one beloved therewhile
Mornstar's rose-rays soft touched her face? Did she weep
    And whisper with longing to leave that pumice isle,
" The waves foam'd amarathine bloom
    As the rose in mine hair, yet fadeless its hue";
And in that twilight hour his fey doom,
        Eyes of blue.

Oft she'd gaze out her whitely keep o'er the main
    For the sight of his sail on the finitor,
The warmth of his beam, 'fore his fathom again,
    Yet in each adieu linger ever tighter.
He always would caress a sanguine rose
    Pressed on her ear as he said his goodbyes;
As he hid his tears, disappear'd below
        Scarlet skies.

On summer's eve—'neath that cypress tree
    Isadora lay at ease whilst the dulcimer play'd
And her Corsair's sweet strains of love's far sea;
    Here she fell upon paradise estray'd:
For the Seraphim wind and the whitening wave
    Washed Isadora on those shores to the rescuing arm
Of her swain; and from knaves with the slash of his glaive,
    Safe from harm.

OF LORE

Her blues o'erlooked the deep's arrest
    Atop that spire where they trothed their vow;
Below a crestfallen moon she was dressed
    In cymar, and her longing grew deeper now.
Down starry stairs in a swoon she stumbled
    To the garden, the moonglade pool, where she placed
On her breast the bloom she held—so crumbled
        That unlaced.

The Corsair's heart deep, to the depths of despair
    When on that Orient shore shone no light
From her bower yet shewn in the twilight air;
    With hast on landing on strands of white
He ran up those grottoed stairs with falcion
    Unsheathed to unleash its fell blade on foe,
But as last footfall, reached the gladed fountain—
        Fell in woe.

O, did tears of a love far deeper than ocean fall here
    At the sight of bosom white whence that tender hand
Last grasp'd the petaled flower of love—held dear
    As held long his angel upon the sand?
And 'held her azure eyes, still'd their liquid fire;
    Her sandy tresses, which fell so long,
Only sways with Zephyrus, who e'er lays on his lyre—
        Her love song.

January 21, 2019

TO LOOK UPON EURYDICE

Isadora

ASPHODEL.

Her song—is echoed in the shrill of sparrows
She's foreshadowed with rhyme
Of rivulets in the fathomed gale:
'Tis Ver, sublime.
O, behold the seventh shrouded heaven!
And the fire of her drum,
And hear the shush of her lullèd hush
Of the storm, to her touch—succumb;
In the meads a-flood with the violet's bud
A maiden reposes at ease,
Whilst naked naiades dance in a trance
Set free from wintery freeze.
On her dais she's crown'd, with circulet round
The green of the living trees.

TO LOOK UPON EURYDICE

She rests by waters, that eternal daughter,
Whilst above is Phaethon's ray;
In the shade of a willowed rill,
She fills her amphora's clay
With the nectar of earth, and pours the liquor
On the last of summer's bloom;
The clouds are all cast of blacken ash
From the fires on the finitor loom;
The stag bestirs in the sylvan myrrh;
Her eyes with a plaintive brook,
Whilst thunderlight in silence lilts,
The portents of paradise shook;
The warm deluge bewets that dale,
Eden of the serpent's rook.

OF LORE

The air of the hallow in music mellow;
On Samhain's soiree beneath
An eldritch yew, in a dress a hue
As the violet bloom of heath,
She dances imbibing last of eventide;
Her lapis eyes as a doe
Affix'd on the sanguine oak, and is pang'd,
As the osiers yellow asway in the meadow,
And the hoof of a steed in the marshy mead,
And the hoot of an eldritch owl.—
Rebellows the lais the wassailers play,
When a horseman appears on the prowl!
On a blackly mare, and she screams in despair
At the rapt of the knave with a scowl.

TO LOOK UPON EURYDICE

Her song's forgotten, an afterthought,
Adrift in the icy dour;
Yet betimes her song is seen on the long
And endarken'd, sorcellèd hour,
In nightertale, when Borea's veil
Astrewns the midnight dome:
Her gown of violet, heaven lit.
And the sprites on the frozen loam,
On their lyres still pluck the melody struck
By the princess who hummed that tune,
Whilst bathing in lilies and daffodilies.
Beneath an Oaken Moon,
On his dais she's crown'd, with circulet bound,
Darken'd Queen—of the Asphodel dune.

April 11, 2021

OF LORE

CLEOPATRA AND HER ANTONY.

Prelude.

THE jewel of the Nile was neither found
    In wuther'd tombs of sand, nor pyramids grand;
    But in a love still told by wand'ring sound,
  Whisper'd where lovers traced the desert strand.
Between the dream and reality of Rome,
    Between the glass and sand befalls their woe,
      Falls Antony, within her amorous art;
        Untouched in ancient tome,
  A tale that's told in shadowland of pharaoh,
    Of a heart, bespell'd by beauty's arching dart.

TO LOOK UPON EURYDICE

Part the First.

Oh! that sweet hour of love, that tend'rest hour—
    When first approach'd her eyes and soft pursued;
When fainly spied her barge, a beauteous flower
    Upon the Cydnus river, deep subdued.
A strangely haze! the mist, her sweet perfume;
    Her galley gleamed as Phoebus' gilded throne;
        Below its purple sail the tuneful flute,
            A siren's song abloom.
The fragrant airs press soft on sailcloth blown,
    By serenaded pipe! the oars in swift pursuit.

Awashed by whispy waves of linens fair,
    Her silken skin, the fairest of complexion,
With lofty cheek bones framed by raven hair;
    Antony's knees weaken'd with love's affection,
As linger'd long on him—those glitt'ring sapphires.
    A circlet coiled above her luminous face,
        Crowned as a temptress cast from paradise;
            On leopard skin retires,
    In secret chamber waits her swains embrace:
        Drawing nigh, coquettish beams her soft entice.

Such beauty! beyond earth or heavens!—lighty
   In bower veiled in silk, a golden hue,
Arrayed in artful glints of Aphrodite;
   Tending her tempting eyes of skiey blue,
Fairy maids, with peacock feathers fann'd;
    Whose wind did touch to tame her features sweet,
      Yet prest to him, prolong'd her longing sighs
        As he kissed soft her hand,
     And smiling pledged his sword, and heart's heartbeat:
    In Cleopatra's arms beneath Cilicia skies.

        Part the Second.
Arrows aflame light laden hulls like candles,
   The murky Ionian sea set ablaze
With Greek fire's fulgent flames and screams of vandals,
   Broken galleys sink in roily haze;
She holds her fragile fate with wanton mouth,
    On Actium's sea-winds her destiny:
      Seeing the rosy sea, its crimson wine—
        " 'Tis done, to warmèd south,
Let's flee to sallow shores—my Antony—"
    Her sunlit face as Love's engravèd shrine.

TO LOOK UPON EURYDICE

A tamarisk bemoans o'er blacken'd strait,
    A distant solemn tune of sorrow's gale;
On finitor saw dim his destined fate,
    Beyond those grottoed shores of teal set sail,
Past flesh and bone, the blue abyss aflame,
    Till last afloat in fragrance, far from violence.—
        Dusk on a drifting mast, the world—it ends
            With Eros' arrowed aim:
    Whilst lone he sits beneath the stars in silence,
        An ink-stained scroll let loose as Rome descends.

On Pharos isle a tower looms above
    The warring waves within that emerald bay;
Atop its stoney spire, a fire for Love,
    Guiding her wand'ring bark, with beckoning ray:
Behold! purpureal sails ripple delight,
    Sonorous singing feigns of victory sweet,
        The decks bedeck'd with lotus flower wreath;
            Yet Antony took flight,
    Bound to the wilderness of dunes and heat:
        No kohl-traced eyes to drink nor balmy oils to breathe.

OF LORE

Part the Third.

A lonely palm leans sway'd, whilst strains entrance
   Harmonious, 'neath Luna's midnight loom—
On desert winds the sound of satyrs dance;
   In twilight sands of white, a windswept tomb
Stands lone, that obelisk stone, with glyphs ornate;
   Beneath the flick'ring of a fading star,
     Great tumult, wassailers drunken wending
        Through Alexandria's gate;
   Afar his thoughts, of omens unaware,
     The Nile's mysterious bosom, blood portending.

An eagle soars the skies and flies below
   On banners red and gold of ancient Rome:
Time ebbs and flows, a river long ago,
   From parchment whispers doom'd what rose from foam,
" Thy queen hast slain herself on evenfall."
   Antony in agony, fell on sword;—
     Yet heard, " She lives! thy Venus of the tides!"
        This is how kingdoms fall,
   Not with sword, but seal on wax outpour'd;
     He gasps, " Take me good friend where Love abides."

TO LOOK UPON EURYDICE

Dawn on a pillared wall, the whiff of perfume,
   Resounds the sea, and seamews winged on air;
Uplook'd to eyes so blue in pallid room,
   Love's last confluence, laid on bosom fair:
Alas! his ache sated with sighing sips,
   " Elysium's white shores, we twain shall rest:—
     O Antony!" bewail'd her agony
       'Twixt waning heart and lips
   As render'd life by asp—held bane to breast:—
    Tragedy!—Cleopatra and her Antony.

March 7, 2016

OF LORE

Cleopatra

TO LOOK UPON EURYDICE

Memories.

I PORE on reveries of lips so soft,
As eyes whose shore doth lie upon my breast;
Her pale surrender ebbs and flows aloft
From the rubescence of her cheeks suggest;
In sleep hear voice my susurrus of rest
As summer winds adrifting sweet woodbine;
O sanguine lips! the last of lighted west
To greet my eye, thy beam, my soul's sunshine.
I miss her still, in the stillness weep and pine:
Drear tears befall my mien—like Dayspring's dew,
Lethe lingers, a drink deep of deeps devine,
Those tawny eyes, whose timid spell I knew.
    Memories past endure the last adieu,
    Though sever'd, heals with hearts review.

THE END.

Acknowledgments

I wish to bestow my deepest thanks to a poet friend, Ferrick Gray: for taking the time to beta-read my poetry, for letting me know which of my poems were the best of these minor works; and for all his invaluable critiques, which helped me become a better poet.

I also wish to mention the numerous portrait photographers on Artstation who gave me permission to buy an extended commercial license to use their photos as a reference for the graphite drawings I created to illustrate a few of my poems. Thank you Grafit Studio, Lia Koltyrina, Howard Lyon, Mels Mneyan, and Jessica Truscott. Also I would like to thank the lovely models who posed for those portraits, without whom my artwork would not have the spark of life that only a real life reference illuminates.

To my editorial team at Reedsy, for finding numerous errs, I would never have spotted, I am eternally grateful. And appreciate taking your time to edit my poetry: Michael Martin for your thorough copy edit, and Fern Beattie for your brilliant proof read, finding several meter mistakes I missed, which only someone with a poetic ear could have found. And, for giving her opinion of whether I should keep the original or recently revised lines of two poems I had been struggling with.

Finally, I wish to thank you the reader for purchasing this small collection of poems. Without your support I would be unable to continue to publish further poetical works. If you like my poetry, please do consider leaving a kind review.

Kindest regards,
KENNETH.

California, February, 2024

About the Author

Kenneth is an artist and poet.
He lives in the idyllic mountains of California.

Made in the USA
Monee, IL
31 January 2025

d86507e8-dc09-43c3-af44-0e9e0de7be0cR01